Anglo-Saxon Attitudes

A Short Introduction to Anglo-Saxonism

J. A. Hilton

Anglo-Saxon Books

Published 2006

Anglo-Saxon Books
Frithgarth
Thetford Forest Park
Hockwold
Norfolk
IP26 4NQ

© J.A. Hilton

PL

British Library Cataloguing-in-Publication Data. A
catalogue record for this book is available from the
British Library.

ISBN 1–898281-39-4

To

My Teachers

He's an Anglo-Saxon Messenger – and those are Anglo-Saxon attitudes. He only does them when he's happy.

Lewis Carroll, *Through the Looking-Glass*

The great thing about history is that it is adaptable.

Sir Peter Ustinov

Contents

Acknowledgements

I am grateful for their help to the Central Library, Manchester, Chetham's Library, Manchester, the John Rylands Library of the University of Manchester, the Portico Library, Manchester, the Athenaeum, Liverpool, and the Talbot Library, Preston, and to Mr John McDermott for his comments on the draft of this book.

Preface

This is a book about Anglo-Saxonism. It is not a book about the Anglo-Saxons, but a book about books about Anglo-Saxons. It describes the academic discipline of Anglo-Saxonism - a body of knowledge about the Anglo-Saxons, and the methods of studying the Anglo-Saxons: philology, literary criticism, history, archaeology, and so on, in other words manifest Anglo-Saxonism – and tries to investigate its underlying assumptions and the uses to which it has been put, in other words, by analogy with Orientalism, latent Anglo-Saxonism. These presuppositions and purposes have changed over time, since the first appearance of Anglo-Saxonism, but right from the start there have been constant themes: English patriotism and English freedom. Over twenty years ago, while walking in the footsteps of George Orwell, along the Leeds-Liverpool Canal in Ince, near Wigan, I came upon a slogan painted on a fence. It read 'ENGLISH NATIONAL LIBERATION ARMY + SE SWA HIS HLAFORD' [Anglo-Saxon for 'each his own lord']. I have been unable to discover anything about the English National Liberation Army but the slogan 'each his own lord' is a statement of individual freedom that might appeal to Lady Thatcher. Some see a dark side to Anglo-Saxonism, believing that it appeals to a narrow nationalism and even to racism. Others see a positive insistence on freedom.

The migration of the Anglo-Saxons to England is a foundation myth. This is not to imply that the story is not based on fact, any more than the foundation stories of the United States of America or the French Republic, but it is to assert the primary importance of the history of the origins of the English. Similarly, the Norman Conquest might be called a destruction myth. These myths help in the construction of the national identity. That identity is both manifold and subject to change. In these times, that identity is being reshaped by the rise of Celtic (Irish, Scots, and Welsh) and English nationalism; and the possible collapse of the United Kingdom, by the creation of the European Union, and by new waves of immigration into England from the widening European Union, the former British Empire and many other parts of the world.

I am aware that the Anglo-Saxons did not call themselves Anglo-Saxons. Some called themselves Angles, for example in East Anglia, and some called themselves Saxons, for example in Wessex. The Romans and the Celts called them Saxons but they tended to call themselves Angles or English. The Germans came to call them Anglo-Saxons to distinguish them from the Saxons who remained in Germany. Similarly, the English called their language neither Anglo-Saxon nor Old English, but simply English. Hence, they called the country they settled in England rather than Anglo-Saxony or New Saxony, though Anglo-Saxony might be a convenient term to cover both England and the lands they came from. Just to confuse the issue, Saxony, whence the Saxons came to England, was on the western coast of Germany. As, however, it lost territory to the north and west and gained it to the south and east, it migrated across Germany, so that it now lies in the south-east of Germany.

I am convinced that the Angles who settled in England were in fact the obtuse Angles. I suspect that they landed here in summer, and hoped that it would warm up and stop raining. Meanwhile, their fellow German barbarians, the Goths, Franks, and Vandals, headed south into Italy, Gaul (now France), Spain, and even North Africa, where they lived like Romans, enjoying the sunshine, the wine, and the olives. The descendants of the Angles are now trying to remedy the error of their ancestors by moving south in increasing droves, either temporarily or permanently to the Costas of Spain, the Auvergne, and Tuscany or Chiantishire. My own personal ambition is a little apartment in Rome.

Before examining the historiography of the Anglo-Saxons, it might be helpful to outline their history. The Anglo-Saxons came from Germany and Jutland, and established themselves in southern Britain, a former province of the Roman Empire, which became England, in the fifth century. The pagan Anglo-Saxons were converted to Catholic Christianity at the end of the sixth century. At the end of the eighth century, the heathen Danes invaded England, established themselves in the Danelaw in eastern England, were converted to Christianity, and were eventually conquered by the English. In the early eleventh century, the kings of Denmark made themselves kings of England. Having briefly recovered its independence, England was conquered by the Normans in 1066.

In writing this book I have been conscious of the ghost of William Barnes leaning over my shoulder and tutting every time I have used a word with a Romance instead of a Germanic root. I have tried to obey his injunctions but confess that I have not been completely successful. Meanwhile, over the other shoulder I could feel the ghosts of William Morris and his master John Ruskin complaining that I was just writing a book about books and urging me to write something that would make the world a better place. If I can persuade my readers to read some of the books that I have read to write this book, then I hope that they might enjoy them as much as I have. In addition, I would argue that one of the most positive aspects of Anglo-Saxonism is democracy, and that democracy is endangered by a lack of due procedure. In *Hereward the Wake* (see chapter 5), Charles Kingsley imagines the Anglo-Danish army debating its course of action with proper respect for due procedure. When I went to grammar school fifty years ago, my father gave me a copy of *Pear's Cyclopedia*. Amongst its many useful contents, was a description of proper democratic procedure. We followed this procedure in meetings at school and at university. When I left university I entered a world where proper procedure was not universally followed. In such cases the results were boredom, chaos, and petty dictatorship. I know that some people are put off by formality, but formal procedure ensures the triumph of the democratic will. In the hope of placating the shades of Morris and Ruskin, therefore, I provide an appendix on democratic procedure.

1. Renaissance Anglo-Saxonism:

Rediscovering Old English and Re-Inventing the English Nation

During the Protestant Reformation of the sixteenth century, Anglo-Saxon was rediscovered and used to help with the re-invention of the English nation. With the Norman Conquest, English had ceased to be a written language. Latin was already the language of the Church, and, together with French, it became the language of government and the law. Fortunately, much literature in English was preserved in manuscripts kept in the monasteries. Meanwhile, spoken English was changing, so that when, at the end of the Middle Ages, it re-emerged as a written language, it was very different from what it had been before the Conquest. As a result, Old English had become incomprehensible. Profound political, religious, and cultural changes, amounting to a re-invention of the English nation, led to the rediscovery of Old English and the use of its literature in this re-invention.

The English Reformation began with **Henry VIII**'s break with the papacy. For a thousand years England had been a Catholic country. Roman and Celtic missionaries had converted the English to Christianity at the end of the sixth century, and the English had accepted the supremacy of the pope as head of the Church. In 1534 an act of parliament declared the king head of the Church of England. Then, between 1536 and 1540, the government dissolved the monasteries, and their precious libraries, including the remains of Old English literature, were almost destroyed. That any manuscripts at all survived was largely due to the single-handed efforts of **John Leland** (c. 1506-1552). Born in Lancashire, he was a scholar educated at Cambridge, Oxford, and Paris, where he came under the influence of the Renaissance, the revival of the Classical learning of ancient Greece and Rome that was sweeping through Europe. He obtained some sort of roving commission from the king to save what manuscripts he could before, perhaps driven to despair by the thought of what he could not save, he went mad a couple of years before his death. Amongst the manuscripts he did save were copies not only of Greek and Latin texts but also of works in Old English.

These Old English manuscripts were at first site incomprehensible. Fortunately, some, such as the Gospels, were translations of Greek and Latin, and some, such as the Anglo-Saxon Chronicle, were already provided with translations into Latin. Accordingly, Old English literature could be understood, and used in support of the Protestant Reformation. The introduction of printing allowed Anglo-Saxon books to be published in large numbers and relatively cheaply. By the reign of Elizabeth I in the second half of the sixteenth century, not only was the Church of England independent of the papacy, but its liturgy was in English, its clergy were no longer celibate, and it had adopted many of the doctrines of continental European Protestantism, such as disbelief in prayers to the saints, in prayers for the dead, and in the real presence of Christ in the Eucharist. The Church's leaders sought justification for these new positions by appealing to the Anglo-Saxon past, and Archbishop Parker of Canterbury began a programme of publishing Anglo-Saxon religious literature in the hope that it would vindicate the Church of England. On the details of Anglo-Saxon religious practice and belief, this hope proved false, for, like it or not, Anglo-Saxon Christians were Roman Catholics, but the controversy rumbled on into the nineteenth century and beyond.

Meanwhile, one of the last surviving glories of Anglo-Saxon England, its Catholic liturgy, was finally destroyed. When **Pope St Gregory** the Great sent **St Augustine** to convert the English to Christianity, he encouraged him to devise a suitable local use or variation of the Roman rite of the Western Church. Augustine combined the austerity of the use of Rome itself with the splendour of the Gallican use of France. Local variations of this use developed in England, but the standard form was the use of Sarum (Salisbury) codified by St Osmund after the Norman Conquest. The **Protestant Reformation** abolished the Old English Use and replaced it with the Book of Common Prayer. The poet **Richard Corbet** lamented the disappearance of the Sarum use:

> By which we note the fairies
> Were of the old profession;
> Their songs were Ave Maries,
> Their dances were procession.

At first the Catholic minority continued to worship following the Sarum use, but its elaborate ceremonies were inappropriate to a persecuted community, and its priests were trained abroad to follow the Roman use. A Catholic attempt to revive it in the nineteenth century failed, but it was adopted by some Anglo-Catholics, and has recently been revived by some Orthodox English-speaking communities. Certain Sarum ceremonies were retained in both the Anglican and the English Roman Catholic liturgies.

England became a Protestant country, but one threatened by Catholic invasion from abroad, such as the Spanish Armada in 1588, and Catholic plots at home, such as that of **Guy Fawkes** in 1605. The Protestant majority of the English saw themselves as a chosen nation, protected by divine providence against the malice of the Catholics. The publication of **Bede**'s *History* in 1643 reinforced this view of the English as God's Chosen People. England was also a country deeply divided between moderate Protestants, Anglicans, who thought that the Reformation had gone far enough, and extreme Protestants, Puritans, who thought that it had not gone far enough, between Royalists, usually Anglicans, who exalted the power of the king, and Parliamentarians, usually Puritans, who exalted the power of parliament, and between the rich, who held political power, and the poor, who did not. The publication of Anglo-Saxon laws in 1568 helped to provide the Parliamentarian revolutionaries with intellectual ammunition in the Civil War, which broke out in 1642. The Parliamentary party argued that the king was not above the law, but rather was subject to it.

The radical revolutionaries, the **Levellers** and **Diggers**, the supporters of the rights of the poor, advocated the theory of the Norman Yoke. During the Conquest, a Norman king and a Norman aristocracy had usurped political power and seized all the land. They believed that, as royal authority had been overthrown, they should go on to redistribute political power and property to the English people. As **Gerard Winstanley** argued:

> The last enslaving yoke that England groaned under (and yet is not freed from) was the Norman, ...and wars, you know presently begun, between the King, that represented William the Conqueror, and the body of the English people that were enslaved ... and William the Conqueror's successor, which was [King] Charles, was cast out; and thereby we have recovered ourselves from under that Norman yoke.

The landowners who controlled parliament, however, were not prepared to surrender power and property, and the Levellers and Diggers were suppressed.

Anglo-Saxonism had been used to help create the English Reformation, and in so doing had, with the English Bible, helped to create the myth of the English as a Chosen People. Amongst the characteristics of this Protestant Chosen People was a God-given freedom, inherited from their Anglo-Saxon ancestors.

2. Enlightened Anglo-Saxonism: Finding English Freedom

During the eighteenth century Anglo-Saxon studies were influenced by and became the vehicle of the ideas of the **Enlightenment**. The publication in 1687 of **Newton's** *Principia Mathematica* demonstrated the triumph of Reason with a capital R. Human reason, more particularly Newton's reason, had been applied to the physical universe and had discovered the laws that governed it. Newton's *Opticks*, published in 1704, provided a metaphor for the process: white light filtered through a prism was broken up into the constituent colours of the rainbow, which were then passed through another prism and re-assembled as white light; reason divided a problem into its parts to understand it and then came up with a simple answer to the whole problem. In 1688 the Divine Right monarchy of the Catholic King **James II** was overthrown in the **Glorious Revolution**, and parliamentary government and religious toleration triumphed. **John Locke** applied Newton's methods to human nature in his *Essay concerning Human Understanding* (1690), and defended parliamentary government in his *Two Treatises on Government* (1690) and religious toleration in his *Letters on Toleration* (1689-92). These ideas were popularised in France by **Voltaire's** *Lettres Philosophiques* (1734). They were taken up by **Montesquieu**, whose *Spirit of the Laws* argued that the structure of society was influenced by environmental factors, such as geography and climate. This complex of ideas was used to understand the history of the Anglo-Saxons, and that history was used to further those ideas.

The groundwork in the study of the Anglo-Saxon language was done by a 'nest of Saxonists' at **Oxford University** in the late seventeenth and early eighteenth centuries. The foundations of learning were the Classics, the literature of ancient Greece and Rome. Boys went to grammar school to learn Latin grammar, and then on to university to study the Classics. As its title implies, Newton's *Principia Mathematica* was written and published in Latin. Classical scholars brought their linguistic

15

skills to the study of Anglo-Saxon. **William Somner** published a dictionary of Anglo-Saxon at Oxford in 1659. **George Hickes** published an Old English grammar in 1689, and then in 1703 he began to publish his *Thesaurus,* a grammar not only of Anglo-Saxon but also of the related Scandinavian languages. Anglo-Saxon materials and some relevant Latin literature were thus available to writers ready to use the methods of the Enlightenment to write English history.

The lead was set by **David Hume** (1711-1776). He was a Scot of the generation that embraced the Act of Union of 1707. His contemporary **Johnson** may have remarked that 'the noblest prospect that a Scotchman ever sees, is the high road that leads him to London', but Hume remained in Edinburgh, helping to make it 'the Athens of the North'. Hume knew that 'all the lowlands ... were peopled in great measure from Germany ... The language, spoken in those countries, which is purely Saxon, is a stronger proof of this event, than can be opposed by the imperfect, or rather fabulous annals, which are obtruded on us by the Scottish historians'. Following the system of Newton and Locke, he was a philosopher who advocated scepticism about anything beyond sense experience, and in particular about religion. He brought the same intellectual rigour to the writing of history. His *History of England,* published between 1754 and 1761, was an outstanding academic and popular success, and from his death it went through another fifty editions by the end of the nineteenth century. It contained the standard account of the Anglo-Saxons.

Hume's work was followed by that of **Edward Gibbon** (1737-1794). His *Decline and Fall of the Roman Empire,* which appeared between 1776 and 1788, dealt with the Anglo-Saxon invasion of Britain. An exponent of the Enlightenment, his ironic survey of the rise of Christianity was deeply critical of its supernatural pretensions. He summed up the decline and fall of the Roman Empire as 'the triumph of barbarism and religion'. Hume and Gibbon derived many of their facts about and a lot of their attitudes to the Anglo-Saxons from the ancient Roman historians.

As the Romans extended their Empire beyond the confines of Italy in the second and first centuries BC, they came into contact with the German tribes, including those that were to become the Anglo-Saxons. **Julius Caesar** clashed with the Germans in Gaul and drove them back beyond the Rhine. In 9 AD, the Emperor **Augustus** attempted to establish a new frontier on the Elbe, by sending Quintilius Varus with three legions, some twenty thousand men, into Germany. They were wiped out in the Teutoberger Forest by a German army commanded by **Arminius or Hermann** the German. Augustus would bang his head on the door-posts, and cry 'Quintilius Varus, give me back my legions!' As a result, the northern Roman frontier was stabilised along the Rhine and Danube, but was under continual and growing pressure from the Germans beyond. Eventually in the fifth century the western Roman Empire collapsed, in 410 **Alaric** and his Goths sacked Rome itself, and the various Germanic nations established themselves within the Roman Empire: the Goths in Italy and Gaul, the Vandals in Africa, the Franks in Gaul, which became France, and the English in Britain. The Goths and Vandals fell to the armies of the Eastern (Byzantine) Roman Empire and to Muslim Arabs, but the Franks and English acquired permanent settlements. However, although the Franks quickly adopted the Christian religion and the Latin language, which eventually became French, the English retained their Germanic heathen religion and language. Although the English were converted to Christianity, they kept their German language.

For the Romans, therefore, the **Germans** were the Other, a dangerous enemy to be feared, hated, and, paradoxically admired. For Julius Caesar, concerned to justify his conduct of the war in Gaul and to magnify his victories, the Germans were 'strong and as tall as giants'. For **Tacitus**, a Roman aristocrat who lived under the corrupt tyrannies of Nero and Domitian, the Germans were noble savages to contrast with his servile and effete fellow Romans. They have 'wild, blue eyes, reddish hair and huge frames that excel only in violent effort'. The Germans are not only courageous but have also retained their liberty and their public and private virtues. Important matters are decided by 'the whole community' assembled in arms. 'No one in Germany finds vice amusing, or calls it "up-to-date" to debauch and be debauched'. Hume and Gibbon relied heavily on Tacitus' 'pencil', which in the eighteenth century meant a brush, a metaphor for his vivid description of Germany. They learnt from him not only about the Germans but also about tyranny, how democratic institutions could be used to mask dictatorship.

The Enlightened historians, committed to reason and liberty, therefore, found in the classical historians not only factual information but also a ready made set of attitudes to which they could add their own, a complex of opposite pairs: civilization and barbarism, despotism and liberty, virtue and vice, and reason and superstition. **Hume** praised German freedom:

> Of all the barbarous nations, ... the Germans seem ... to have carried to the highest pitch the virtues of valour and love of liberty ... the sovereign ... was directed in every measure by the common consent of the nation ... the inferior leaders ... were elected by the votes of the people ...

The Saxons, however, were the most barbarous of the Germans: 'one of the most warlike tribes of this fierce people, and had become the terror of the neighbouring nations'. In Britain they 'threw everything back into ancient barbarity; and those few natives, who were neither massacred nor expelled their habitations, were reduced to the most abject slavery'. For Hume the conversion of the English to Christianity was merely the triumph of superstition over ignorance. St Augustine:

> attracted their attention by the austerity of his manners, by the severe penances to which he subjected himself, by the abstinence and self-denial which he practised: and having excited their wonder by a course of life, which appeared so contrary to nature, he procured more easily their belief of miracles, which, it was pretended, he wrought for their conversion.

Hume even blames Christianity for the success of the invading Danes, who were able 'by sudden inroads, to make great progress over a people, who were not defended by any naval force, who had relaxed their military institutions, and who were sunk into a superstition, which had become odious to the Danes and ancient Saxons ...'. Meanwhile, the Saxons

> imported into this island the same principles of independence, which they had inherited from their ancestors. ... The language was pure Saxon ... the manners and customs were wholly German ... and the same picture of a fierce and bold liberty, which is drawn by the masterly pencil of Tacitus, will suit those founders of the English government.

This free government was overthrown by the Norman Conquest, and 'Except the former conquest of England by the Saxons themselves, who were induced, by peculiar circumstances, to proceed even to the extermination of the natives, it would be difficult to find in all history a revolution more destructive, or attended with a more complete subjection of the ancient inhabitants'.

Gibbon devotes a chapter to the description of ancient Germany, because of the role of the Germans in the fall of the Roman Empire and because

> The most civilised nations of modern Europe issued from the woods of Germany, and in the rude institutions of those barbarians we may still distinguish the original principles of our present laws and manners. In their primitive state of simplicity and independence the Germans were surveyed by the discerning eye, and delineated by the masterly pencil, of Tacitus, the first of historians who applied the science of philosophy to the study of facts.

In particular, 'an Englishman may curiously trace the establishment of the barbarians from whom he derives his name, his laws, and perhaps his origin.' He describes the Saxons as 'warlike barbarians'. Accordingly, 'The arms and religion, the laws and language, which the Romans had so carefully planted in Britain were extirpated by their barbarous successors. ...The language of science, of business, and of conversation, which had been introduced by the Romans, was lost in the general desolation ... those illiterate Pagans preserved and established the use of their national dialect'. Gibbon at least acquits the Saxons of the charge of genocide:

> This strange alteration has persuaded historians, and even philosophers, that the provincials of Britain were totally exterminated ... but neither reason nor facts can justify the unnatural supposition that the Saxons of Britain remained alone in the desert which they had subdued. After the sanguinary barbarians had secured their dominion and gratified their revenge, it was their interest to preserve the peasants, as well as the cattle, of the unresisting country.

As for the Norman Conquest he remarked that 'Under the yoke of the Norman conquest, the Danes and English were oppressed and united', but 'England was assuredly a gainer by the conquest'.

For Hume and Gibbon, as for Tacitus, the Saxons were the Other. Steeped in the values of Classical civilisation, they looked back from the Olympian calm of the Enlightenment at a barbarous and superstitious people. They knew how thin was the crust of civilisation, how continually it was threatened by barbarism and superstition, but they also saw in the Saxons the origins of the freedom they enjoyed.

3. Romantic Anglo-Saxonism: Seeking National Reconciliation

The Enlightened historians had looked back and down on the Anglo-Saxons, but a new generation of writers looked back and across to them without condescension. Indeed, they idealised their Anglo-Saxon past. It was this point of view, rather than any cult of nature, of sentiment, or of individual genius, which allows us to call these writers Romantic. (Of course, strictly speaking 'Romantic Anglo-Saxonism' is a contradiction in terms, since 'Romantic' refers to languages derived from Latin rather that the Germanic languages, but 'Romantic' has come to refer to this idealisation of the early middle ages.) At a time of violent economic, social, and political upheaval, the Romantic Anglo-Saxonists recalled the English to their Anglo-Saxon roots, whilst, like their Enlightened predecessors, exalting the values of freedom and tolerance.

The turn of the eighteenth and nineteenth centuries was the beginning of what Professor **Hobsbawm** has called 'the Age of Revolution', 'the "dual revolution" – the French Revolution of 1789 and the contemporaneous (British) Industrial Revolution'. People flocked from the countryside to work long hours in harsh conditions, while technological improvements or changes in the markets occasionally threw them out of work, and they lived crowded together in insanitary conditions. Political power was in the hands of the landed aristocracy and gentry. The French declared their intention of spreading the Revolution, with its ideals of Liberty, Equality, and Fraternity, throughout Europe. Between 1793 and 1815 Britain was continually at war with Revolutionary and Napoleonic France. English Radicals called for Revolution here, and the government reacted with measures to curb freedom of speech and assembly. Discontent and repression continued after the war, culminating in the Peterloo Massacre in Manchester in 1819. The Radical leader **Tom Paine** declared that as a result of the Norman Conquest 'the Nation runs in the line of being conquered, and it ought to rescue itself from this reproach'. The pretensions of the newly-rich middle classes were satisfied by giving them the vote in the Reform Act of 1832, but the demands of the **Chartists** for a democratic constitution were refused, despite revived fears of revolution in 1848, the Year of Revolution throughout Europe. There was, however, no political revolution in England, and the Romantic Anglo-Saxonists preached national reconciliation.

For the first time since Bede, histories were written exclusively devoted to the Anglo-Saxons. As a boy, **Sharon Turner** (Sharon now a female name was then male) read the 'Death-Song of Ragnar Lodbrok' (published in Percy's *Five Pieces of Runic Poetry*), and it inspired him to dedicate his life to the study of Anglo-Saxon and Viking antiquities. He lived close to the British Museum, where he spent his leisure studying Old English manuscripts. The result was his *History of England from the earliest period to the Norman Conquest*, published between 1799 and 1825. It was a thorough and detailed account of Anglo-Saxon history and society. **John Lingard** was a Catholic priest, whose *The Antiquities of the Anglo-Saxon Church* demonstrated conclusively that the Anglo-Saxon Church was a Roman Catholic Church, which was partly founded by the pope and accepted papal supremacy, ground he covered again in the first volume of his *History of England*. **Daniel Rock** was another Catholic priest, whose *The Church of our Fathers* was a detailed account of the use of Sarum, which he hoped to revive, because it 'was so very Anglo-Saxon'. **Sir Francis Palgrave** was of Jewish extraction and originally named Cohen. His *History of the Anglo-Saxons*, published in 1831, argued that the ancient Britons were not Celtic but Germanic.

Macaulay's *History of England*, published between 1848 and 1861, was a popular success and became a classic. Thomas Babington Macaulay (1800-1859) was a successful politician. As a Member of Parliament, he was a leading supporter of the Reform Act of 1832. As a member of the Supreme Council of India, he established English as the official language of India. He became Lord Macaulay two years before his death, and he is buried in Westminster Abbey. In his *History*, though it concentrated on the period between 1685 and 1702, he maintained that 'the history of our country during the last hundred and sixty years is eminently the history of physical, of moral, and of intellectual improvement'. It dealt briefly with the Anglo-Saxons in its opening pages, explaining how Saxons and Danes were reconciled by intermarriage and by religion so that 'The Danish and Saxon tongues, both dialects of one widespread language, were blended together', and how Anglo-Danes and Normans were reconciled under King John, when:

> The two races so long hostile, soon found that they had common interests and common enemies ... The great grandsons of those who had fought under William and the great grandsons of those who had fought under Harold began to draw near to each other in friendship; and the first pledge of their reconciliation was the Great Charter, won by their united exertions, and framed for their common benefit ... In no country has the enmity of race been carried further than in England. In no country has that enmity been more completely effaced.

Another instant success that became a classic was **Sir Walter Scott**'s *Ivanhoe*, published in 1819, the year of the Peterloo Massacre, advocating national reconciliation. Scott (1771-1832) virtually invented the historical novel, and his works are classics still in print. Set during the reign of Richard I at the end of the twelfth century, *Ivanhoe* describes the divisions between the Anglo-Saxons and their Norman rulers:

> A circumstance, which greatly tended to enhance the tyranny of the nobility and the sufferings of the inferior classes, arose from the consequences of the Conquest by Duke William of Normandy. Four generations had not sufficed to blend the hostile blood of the Normans and Anglo-Saxons, or to unite, by common language and mutual interests, two hostile races, one of which felt the elation of triumph, while the other groaned under the consequences of defeat.

The English jester, Wamba, sums up the situation in a song:

> Norman saw on English oak,
> On English neck a Norman yoke:
> Norman spoon in English dish,
> And England ruled as Normans wish;
> Blithe world to England never will be more,
> Till England's rid of all the four.

The England of *Ivanhoe* is riven by mutual hatred: villainous Normans, led by Prince John, against gallant Anglo-Saxons, led by the eponymous Ivanhoe and Robin Hood; Normans and Anglo-Saxons are, except for Ivanhoe, united in hatred of the Jews, represented by Rebecca and her father Isaac; and Ivanhoe, because he has adopted the Norman method of fighting on horseback and entered the service of King Richard, is divided from his father, Cedric, a fanatical English patriot, who refuses to let Ivanhoe marry his ward Rowena. Ivanhoe is helped by Isaac and Rebecca. Prince John's henchmen kidnap Cedric, Rowena, Isaac, and Rebecca, but Ivanhoe, Robin Hood, and King Richard rescue all but Rebecca, who becomes the prisoner of the fanatical Master of the Templars. Ivanhoe saves Rebecca from being burned as a witch, is reconciled to his father, and married to his Rowena. As a result,

> these distinguished nuptials were celebrated by high-born Normans, as well as Saxons, joined with the universal jubilee of the lower orders, that marked the marriage of two individuals as a pledge of the future peace and harmony betwixt two races, which, since that period, have been so completely mingled, that the distinction has become wholly invisible.

Scott saw how fanatical devotion to a cause, however noble, could blind people to humanity. He knew that, although one can sacrifice oneself to a cause, one has no right to sacrifice others. *Ivanhoe* is Scott's plea for tolerance and humanity.

Macaulay and Scott, the historian and the novelist, called for national reconciliation at a time of profound and rapid change. They appealed to the ruling classes, represented by the Normans, and the people, represented by the Anglo-Saxons, to work together at a time when many feared or, in the case of Marx and Engels, hoped for revolution.

4. Germanic Anglo-Saxonism: Finding the Roots of Language

While Romantic historians and novelists were preaching national reconciliation in England during the Age of Revolution, English and Continental scholars were making fundamental discoveries about the nature of language and inventing the discipline of philology, the love of language. At the same time, they discovered *Beowulf,* which English, Danes, and Germans, all claimed as their national epic.

Students of language were aware that in Western Europe there were groups of related languages, which had developed from common sources. During the Middle Ages, Latin had given birth to Italian, French, and Spanish. Thus 'pater', the Latin word for 'father', had changed into 'padre' in both Italian and Spanish and into 'pere' in French. Latin is also related to Greek; the Greek for 'father' is also 'pater'. The English came from Germany, so the German for 'father' is 'vater', while in Dutch it is 'vader' and in Old English it is 'faeder'.

Similarities even further afield were noticed by **Sir William Jones**, Chief Justice of Bengal. From the middle of the eighteenth century to the middle of the nineteenth, the English were engaged in the conquest of India. English administrators studied Indian languages, including Sanskrit, its ancient sacred language. In a paper delivered to the Asiatic Society in 1786 Jones observed:

> The Sanskrit language, whatever be its antiquity, is of a wonderful structure; more perfect than the Greek, more copious than the Latin, and more exquisitely refined than either, yet bearing to both of them a stronger affinity, both in the roots of the verbs and in the forms of grammar, than could possibly have been produced by accident; so strong, indeed, that no philologer could examine them all three, without believing them to have sprung from some common source, which, perhaps, no longer exists.

The implications of Jones's insight were worked out by scholars in Denmark and Germany, both countries profoundly affected by the Napoleonic Wars. Denmark sided with France. The English defeated the Danish fleet at Copenhagen in 1801 (Nelson putting his telescope to his blind eye, and declaring 'Signal, what signal? I see no signal'.), and then bombarded the city and captured the entire Danish fleet in 1807. As a result, by the Treaty of Kiel in 1814, Denmark surrendered Norway, which was annexed by Sweden. Although Denmark retained the Norwegian dependencies of the Faeroes, Iceland, and Greenland, it ended the wars deeply humiliated. Germany was a collection of independent kingdoms and principalities, all of which were forced at some time or other to co-operate with France, though others like Austria and Prussia were more or less consistent enemies of France. Despite taking a beating by the French, at least Austria and Prussia ended up on the winning side.

German scholars were inspired by the Romantic Sturm und Drang (Storm and Stress) philosophy of **Herder**. In 1769 he sailed from German-speaking Riga in Russian Livonia, where he had been teaching, to Nantes in France. In his *Journal of My Voyage in the Year 1769* he characterised himself as rootless, seeking to understand the future through studying the past. The sea-voyage, by bringing him close to simple men dependent upon nature, had given him 'experience to illuminate the original era of myths', which expressed the concerns of ordinary folk (Volk).

Rasmus Rask was a Dane who helped to lay the foundations of philology. He was a librarian at the University of Copenhagen, and was eventually promoted to professor. He was a man of formidable learning, mastering twenty-five languages and dialects and studying twice as many. In 1811 he published the first systematic grammar of Old Norse. He spent the years 1813 to 1815 in Iceland, studying its language and customs, and writing his *Investigation of the Origin of the Old Norse or Icelandic Language,* comparing the Scandinavian languages to Latin and Greek, and showing that the Celtic languages belonged to the same family. He pointed out that the consonants of Germanic languages vary regularly from those of related languages. He published an Anglo-Saxon grammar in 1817, and edited the *Poetic Edda* and the *Prose Edda*, the medieval accounts of Norse myth. He then turned his attention to Indic languages, and travelled to Persia, India, and Ceylon, collecting manuscripts. Rask's scholarship was brought to England in 1830 by Benjamin Thorpe, who had been his student at Copenhagen. Thorpe published an English translation of Rask's *Anglo-Saxon Grammar* in 1830, translated Caedmon in 1832 and *Beowulf* in 1855, published his *Northern Mythology* in 1851, and edited *The Anglo-Saxon Chronicle* in 1861.

Meanwhile **Franz Bopp**, who became professor of Oriental literature and general philology at the University of Berlin, took up Jones's suggestion of the importance of Sanskrit, and established the existence of the Indo-European group of languages. His *On the System of Conjugation in Sanskrit* (1816) attempted to trace the common origin of Sanskrit, Persian, Greek, Latin, and German. His *Comparative Grammar of Sanskrit, Zend, Greek, Latin, Lithuanian, Old Slavic, Gothic, and German* (1833-52) described their grammar and attempted to explain their phonetic laws. He even turned his attention to the languages of Malaysia and Polynesia.

Jacob Grimm made the fundamental breakthrough. He and his brother **Carl** were librarians at Cassel (Kassel) and then at Gottingen. Together they produced their famous collection of *Fairy Tales* (1812-1822), inspired by the theories of Herder, and they were published in an English translation as early as 1824-26 to darken the imagination of generations of English children. Jacob also published his *German Grammar* (1819-37), in fact a Germanic grammar, in which he laid down the natural laws of sound change, demonstrating systematically Rask's principle of the regularity of consonants in related languages, hence known as Grimm's Law; for example, when a word begins with the consonant b or p in Latin, it becomes f or v in Germanic, and vice versa, thus 'pater' becomes 'vater' or 'father', and 'frater' becomes 'bruder' or 'brother'. By examining these sound changes it was possible to get back to the lost original Indo-European language of the Aryan ancestors of the Germans. He went on to publish his *German*

Mythology, arguing that folk stories and heroic legends contained the elements of ancient German heathenism hidden by 'the blighting touch of Christianity'. The brothers also embarked on the preparation of a German dictionary so massive in its scope that it was only completed in the twentieth century. By studying German language and German myth, Grimm hoped to revive the soul of the German people.

At the same time and under the same impulse, the epics of medieval Germany were being revived. The lawyer **Karl Joseph Simrock**, having been removed from office for his support of the French Revolution of 1830, devoted himself to the study of German literature, and published a modern German version of the *Nibelungenlied*, the tragic tale of Siegfried and the dragon's gold. **Karl Lachmann**, professor at the Friedrich Wilhelm University in Berlin laid down the rules of textual criticism, but also sought to go beyond the written text to the oral tradition, which he believed lay behind it and contained an account of historical events. Thus the *Nibelungenlied* written about the year 1200 purported to recount events, which took place in the fifth century during the wandering of the nations.

These developments were welcomed enthusiastically by **Thomas Carlyle** (1795-1881), a Scot, who communicated them to the English public. Of the *Nibelungenlied,* he declared 'if the primeval rudiments of it have the antiquity assigned to them, it belongs to us English *Teutones* as well as the Germans'. He devoted the first part of his *On Heroes, Hero-Worship and the Heroic in History,* first published in 1840, *to* a study of Odin and Odinism. He remarked that Scandinavian heathenism 'is interesting also as the creed of our fathers: the men whose blood still runs in our veins, whom doubtless we still resemble in so many ways'. 'Is it', he went on, 'as the half-dumb stifled voice of the long-buried generations of our own Fathers, calling out of the depths of ages to us in whose veins their blood still runs?'. He concluded:

> Neither is there no use in *knowing* something about this old Paganism of our Fathers. Unconsciously and combined with higher things, it is in *us* yet, that old Faith withal! To know it consciously, bring us into closer and clearer relation with the Past – with our own possessions in the Past.

Meanwhile, the Anglo-Saxon epic *Beowulf* was rediscovered. It survived in only one manuscript and had barely escaped destruction by fire. In 1705 **Humphrey Wanley** in his catalogue of Anglo-Saxon manuscripts described it as about 'Beowulf the Dane'. This description came to the notice of the royal archivist of Denmark, **Grimur Jonsson Thorkelin**, an Icelander, who came to England and transcribed the poem. Unfortunately his work was delayed by the English bombardment of Copenhagen, but he published it in 1815 at the end of the Napoleonic Wars as *About the Deeds of the Danes: A Danish Poem in the Anglo-Saxon Dialect.* Although *Beowulf's* setting was Scandinavia, its language was Old English, and it was, therefore, also possible to claim it as an English national epic.

This great hoard of Germanic literature and scholarship was brought back to England by **John Mitchell Kemble**. He was born in 1805 into a distinguished theatrical family: his father was the actor-manager John Kemble, his aunt Mrs Siddons, and his sister the actress and author Fanny Kemble. He went to Germany in 1828, then to Trinity College, Cambridge, where he was a member of the Apostles, a group of students interested in the arts and politics, and a friend of Tennyson. Kemble returned to Germany in 1833 to Gottingen to sit at the feet of the Grimms. In the same year he returned to England and published an edition of *Beowulf,* which he dedicated to Jacob Grimm, who 'has converted etymological researches ... into a logical and scientific system'. He also published a massive collection of Anglo-Saxon historical sources, and then went on to publish his *The Saxons in England* in 1849.

Kemble dedicated *The Saxons in England* to Queen Victoria, describing it as 'This History of the principles which have given her empire its pre-eminence among the nations of Europe'. He went on to explain that it was:

> An account of the principles upon which the public and political life of our Anglo-Saxon forefathers was based, and of the institutions in which these principles were most clearly manifested ... it is the history of the childhood of our own age, - the explanation of its manhood.

1848 was the Year of Revolution in Europe, but, despite the Chartist agitation, there was no revolution in England. Contrasting the stability of England with the Continent – 'On every side of us thrones totter, and the deep foundations of society are convulsed' - Kemble argued that in England 'our customs are founded upon right and justice', uniting 'the completest obedience to the law with the greatest amount of individual freedom'. He believed Anglo-Saxon institutions 'to be worthy of investigation from their bearing upon the times in which we live … We have a share in the past, and the past yet works in us …'. For Kemble, the study of the Anglo-Saxon past was a means of understanding the English present.

Anglo-Saxon studies had been transformed by Continental scholarship in the lands whence the Anglo-Saxons came. Texts were published and subjected to rigorous analysis, whilst the various Germanic languages and those of the wider Indo-European family were placed into systematic relationship. Kemble brought these achievements back to England, and, like the Grimms, used them to cast the light of the past on his own troubled times.

5. Democratic Anglo-Saxonism: Confirming English Freedom

During the second half of the nineteenth century Anglo-Saxonism justified the increasing democratisation of English politics. Scholarly and popular histories emphasised the democratic nature of Anglo-Saxon society, and historical fiction glorified English resistance to foreign tyranny. Meanwhile, England looked increasingly askance at the increasing power of a newly unified Germany. Perhaps because of this hostility, Anglo-Saxonism was combined with a growing strain of Nordicism, which emphasised the positive role of the Vikings in the creation of England.

The working-classes continued to agitate for full political rights, and successive governments gave way to their demands. In 1867 the **Second Reform Act** effectively gave the vote to the urban working class. It was carried through by the Conservative government of **Disraeli**, who as early as 1845 had asked if it would be Queen Victoria's 'proud destiny to bear relief to suffering millions, and ... break the last links in the chain of Saxon thraldom'. The **Reform Act** of 1884 extended the franchise to the rural working class. The County Councils Act of 1888 created democratic local government outside the boroughs and cities on the basis of the old Anglo-Saxon shires.

At the same time a united, and democratic, Germany was being created from the thirty-odd independent states that made up the German Confederation. It began as the Zollverein, a customs union, common market, or economic community. The prelude to the political unification was a war in 1864 between the German Confederation and Denmark over the duchies of Schleswig and Holstein. (Lord Palmerston remarked that only three people ever understood the Schleswig-Holstein Question: one was dead, one was mad, and himself who had forgotten it.) The Danes appealed to England for help, but despite the recent marriage of

Princess Alexandra of Denmark to the Prince of Wales, the British government decided not to intervene. Following the Austro-Prussian War, the North German Federation was established in 1867. After the Franco-Prussian War, the German Empire was created in 1871. Meanwhile **Wagner** was dramatising the *Nibelungenlied* and setting it to music as his operatic cycle *The Ring of the Nibelungs*. By the turn of the century, England found herself isolated in the Boer War, and Germany was seen as the main threat to our security; in his novel *The Riddle of the Sands,* published in 1903, **Erskine Childers** identified that threat as coming directly from the same creeks of the German coast from which our Anglo-Saxon forefathers had come.

The clash between Denmark and Germany was the background to the career of **George Stephens** (1813-95), 'the runic archaeologist'. The son of a Methodist minister and the brother of another, he became interested in English dialects. His brother at work in Denmark encouraged him to take an interest in Scandinavian languages, and he decided that English was a Scandinavian rather than a German language. He went to Stockholm in 1834 where he founded the Society for the Publication of Ancient Swedish Texts in 1843. He then moved to Copenhagen in 1851, where he became successively lector in English, lector in Anglo-Saxon, and professor of English and Anglo-Saxon, and adopted Danish nationality. He signed himself 'An English Scandinavian'. His *The Old Northern Runic Monuments of Scandinavia and England* (1866-84) set out to prove that English was a Scandinavian language, and that both Schleswig and Holstein were Danish rather than German. For this and other work he was rewarded with knighthoods from all three Scandinavian monarchies: the Order of the Daneborg from Denmark, of St Olaf from Norway (then united with Sweden), and of the Northern Star from Sweden.

William Barnes's love of his native Wessex dialect made him call for English to return to its Anglo-Saxon roots. Poet, schoolmaster, and Anglican clergyman, Barnes (1801-86) was a largely self-taught but immensely learned philologist, who knew seventy languages and was fluent in fourteen. He published *Se Gefylsta,* an Anglo-Saxon primer, in 1849, a *Philological Grammar* in 1854, *Early England and the Saxon-English* in 1869, and *An Outline of Speech-Craft* in 1878. He believed that

> We cannot wonder at the purity of the western dialects, as we must see that the minds of the rustic families of west Saxony, the proper title of the contracted 'Wessex' were as little exposed to the leaven of the old French of the Norman court, as they have been in later times to that of the Latin of the learned, or the so-thought elegant French of the polite ... and so ... the wood-girt and hill-sheltered tuns (or country-houses) of the West were still vocal with the purest Saxon in which the Norman Conquest itself was recorded in the Saxon Chronicle.

He wished to return Standard English, or as Barnes called it 'Englandish', to that Saxon purity. It was not just that he accepted the stylistic injunction to prefer the word of Anglo-Saxon origin to the one borrowed from a foreign language, but that he wished to substitute Anglo-Saxon words for all such borrowings:

> ... as an Englishman, I am sorry that we have not a language of our own; but that whenever we happen to conceive a thought above that of a plough-boy or produce anything beyond a pitch-fork, we are obliged to borrow a word from others before we can utter it, or give it a name.

The solution was to form new words from Anglo-Saxon roots:

> We want ... a pure, homely, strong Saxon-English of English stems, such as would be understood by common English minds and touch English hearts ... We should not reach the English mind or heart the more readily by turning 'He scattered his foes' into 'He dissipated his inimical forces'.

Barnes, therefore, recreated Saxon English by breaking down vocabulary into its component parts of roots, prefixes and suffixes. Thus 'predict' becomes 'foretell', and 'evoke' becomes 'call out'. Sometimes he revived an obsolete word such as 'winsome' or used a dialect word such as 'lonesome'. This process was used, for instance, in contemporary German and Norwegian with official approval and popular support. Barnes, however, was 'a prophet without honour in his own country'. Occasionally he was successful, as with the above, but too often his coinings failed to become current, so we still use 'democracy' rather than 'folkdom' and 'bus' (short for the Latin 'omnibus') rather than my favourite 'folkwain'.

Edward Augustus Freeman's monumental six-volume *History of the Norman Conquest* was a lament for the fall of Anglo-Saxon England. Freeman (1823-92) had the private income to devote himself to independent scholarship, though he was eventually appointed regius professor of history at Oxford, and he preferred to assemble books about himself rather than use a public library. He was a man of narrow views and furious prejudices, believing that 'History is past politics, and politics is present history', dedicated to the Germanic origins of English freedom and to animal welfare, an opponent of the teaching of modern history and of English literature, and unfortunately a virulent anti-Semite. One of the many bees in his bonnet was that the battle of Hastings should be called the battle of 'Senlac', and he quarrelled with the editor of the *Dictionary of National Biography* because he insisted on calling Athelstan *Æthelstan*.

Freeman began his *History of the Norman Conquest* with the assertion that 'The Norman Conquest is the great turning point in the history of the English nation', but that 'So far from being the beginning of our national history, the Norman Conquest was the temporary overthrow of our national being. But it was only a temporary overthrow'. He believed that before the Conquest the English were 'a free and armed people, in whom it is clear that the ultimate sovereignty resides', and, therefore, 'Let him [the historian] go as far back as history or tradition throws any light on the institutions of our race, and he will find the germs alike of the monarchic, the aristocratic, and the democratic branches of our constitution'.

Whilst Freeman devoted six volumes to the tragedy of the Norman Conquest, his friend **John Richard Green** (1837-83) swept through English history from the fifth to the nineteenth century in two slim volumes entitled *A Short History of the English People*. Green was ordained a clergyman of the Church of England, and he served in the slums of London, where he seems to have contracted tuberculosis. After nine years parochial work his health finally broke down, but the Archbishop of Canterbury kindly appointed him to the sinecure of librarian at his Lambeth Palace, allowing Green to spend his winters abroad in the sunshine. His amateur historical studies brought him into contact with Freeman, and, despite their differences they became firm friends, helping one another with their historical writing and travelling together to France and Italy.

Green, like his friend and mentor, Freeman, saw the origins of English freedom in 'the fatherland of the English race' in the Jutland peninsula, amongst 'these English folk in this Old England'. He argued that

> their political and social organization must have been that of the German race to which they belonged. The basis of their society was the free landholder ... The actual sovereignty within the settlement resided in the body of its freemen. Their homesteads clustered round a moot-hill, or round a sacred tree, where the whole community met to administer its own justice and to frame its own laws. ... Here, too, the "witan," the Wise Men of the village, met to settle questions of peace and war, to judge just judgement, and frame wise laws, as their descendants, the Wise Men of a later England, meet in Parliament at Westminster, to frame laws and do justice for the great empire which has sprung from this little body of farmer-commonwealths in Sleswick.

William Morris (1834-96) was primarily a designer, whose work is still profoundly influential – 'If you want a golden rule that will fit everybody, this is it: *Have nothing in your houses that you do not know to be useful, or believe to be beautiful*' – but he was also an eloquent writer and a pioneer Socialist. Morris's Socialism looked backed to these primitive Anglo-Saxon commonwealths for inspiration:

What I mean by Socialism is a condition of society in which there should be neither rich nor poor, neither master nor master's man, neither idle nor overworked, neither brain-sick workers nor heart-sick workers, in a word, in which all men would be living in equality of condition, and would manage their affairs unmasterfully, and with the full consciousness that harm to one would mean harm to all – the realization at last of the word commonwealth.

Morris studied Old Norse and the Norse sagas, and visited Iceland in 1871. 'If a chap can't compose an epic poem while he's weaving tapestry,' he declared, 'he had better shut up, he'll never do any good at all'. He called the *Volsung Saga,* the Old Norse version of the story of the Nibelungs, 'the Great Story of the North, which should be to all our race what the Tale of Troy was to the Greeks'. When he tried to interest Rossetti in the *Volsung Saga,* Rossetti remarked 'I never cared for all that stuff ... How can one take a real interest in a man who has a dragon for a brother?', to which Morris replied 'I'd much rather have a dragon for a brother than a bloody fool', an allusion to Rossetti's brother. Morris translated the *Volsung Saga* into English in 1877:

> O hearken ye who speak the English Tongue,
> How in a waste land ages long ago –
> The very heart of the North bloomed into song
> After long brooding o'er this tale of woe!
> Hearken, and marvel, how it might be so,
> How such a sweetness so well crowned could be
> Betwixt the ice-hills and the cold grey sea.
> ...
> So draw ye round and hearken, English Folk,
> Unto the best tale pity ever wrought,
> Of how from dark to dark bright Sigurd broke,
> Of Brynhild's glorious soul by love distraught,
> Of Gudrun's weary wandering unto naught,
> Of utter Love defeated utterly,
> Of grief too strong to give Love time to die.

A much more popular and enduring evocation of Nordicism was **Charles Kingsley**'s *Hereward the Wake,* first published in 1866 and still in print. Kingsley (1819-75) was another Anglican clergyman, a founding father of the Christian Socialist movement, which brought Christian morality to engage with the social questions created by industrialisation, and a supporter of Darwin's theories of evolution and natural selection. His political and intellectual radicalism did not exclude him from promotion within the Establishment, for he became chaplain to Queen Victoria, a canon of Westminster, and professor of modern history at Cambridge. He turned from writing novels about contemporary social issues to producing historical fiction, including his last novel *Hereward the Wake*, 'the last of the old English' or rather the last of the Anglo-Danes, who held longest against the Norman Conquest. Quite early in the book is that rare thing for a historian, the generous acknowledgement that on a controversial question he was wrong and his opponent, Freeman, was right.

Kingsley maintains that

> ... the men of the Danelagh (*sic*) ...not knowing, like true Englishmen, when they were beaten ... never really bent their necks to the Norman yoke: they kept alive in their hearts that proud spirit of independence, which they brought with them from the moors of Denmark and the dales of Norway; and they kept alive, too, though in abeyance for a while those free institutions which were without doubt the germs of our British liberty.

He describes the Anglo-Danish forces gathered together at Ely:

> They spoke like free Danes; the betters from the upper end of the hall, but every man as he chose. They were in full Thing; in parliament, as their forefathers had been wont to be for countless ages. Their House of Lords and their House of Commons were not yet defined from each other: but they knew the rules of the house, the courtesies of debate; and, by practice of free speech, had educated themselves to bear and forbear, like gentlemen.

Anglo-Saxonism had permeated the consciousness of literate English people, adults and children, for it to be the subject of the gentle satire of **Lewis Carroll**, the pen-name of Charles Lutwidge Dodgson (1832-98). Dodgson was an Anglican clergyman and a fellow of Christ Church, Oxford. His *Alice's Adventures in Wonderland* (1865) was written to amuse Alice Liddell, the daughter of the dean of Christ Church. Together with its sequel *Through the Looking-Glass and What Alice Found There* (1871) it was and remains immensely popular with children and adults.

The poem 'Jabberwocky' in *Through the Looking-Glass* has its Anglo-Saxon elements. As Alice says "'it's all in some language I don't know'", and at first it appears to be written in some kind of Gothic script, "'Why, it's a Looking-glass book, of course! And if I hold it up to a glass, the words will all go the right way again'". It begins and ends with a stanza reminiscent of Anglo-Saxon alliteration:

> Twas brillig, and the slithy toves
> Did gyre and gimble in the wabe;
> All mimsy were the borogroves,
> And the mome raths outgrabe.

Of course, the hero of the poem is Beowulf and the Jabberwock is Grendel.

In *Through the Looking-Glass* the hare in *Alice in Wonderland* becomes Haigha the Messenger, who 'kept skipping up and down, and wriggling like an eel, as he came along, with his great hands spread out like fans on each side', because "'He's an Anglo-Saxon Messenger – and those are Anglo-Saxon attitudes'...'". Carroll's original illustrator, Tenniell, dresses Haigha in Anglo-Saxon costume and makes him gesticulate like a figure in an Anglo-Saxon manuscript.

Rudyard Kipling's *Puck of Pook's Hill* (1906) and its sequel *Rewards and Fairies* (1910) were also enduringly popular children's books and they dealt seriously with the Anglo-Saxons, celebrating reconciliation with the Norman conquerors. Kipling (1865-1936) had experience of belonging to a conquering race. He was born of English parents at

Bombay (Mumbai) in India, where he spent the first few years of his life, and whither, after an education in England, he returned to work as a journalist. His novels and poems of Indian life made him rich and famous, and in 1889 he returned to live in England.

In *Puck of Puck's Hill*, the beginnings of the Anglo-Saxon invasion of Britain are described from the perspective of a Roman officer on Hadrian's Wall, rather like a British officer on the North-West Frontier of India. Kipling has the Norman Sir Richard say of England, as many Englishmen could say of India, "'I set out to conquer England ... I did not know England would conquer me'". Sir Richard's lord De Aquila says "'In God's good time ... there will be neither Saxon nor Norman in England'", and even "'I am not Norman ... nor Saxon ... English am I'". Kipling maintains, however, in the words of Puck that "'The Custom of Old England was here before your Norman knights came, and it outlasted them, though they fought against it cruel'". Kipling sums up this tradition of Saxon democracy in his poem *Norman and Saxon (A.D. 1100)*:

> The Saxon is not like us Normans. His manners are not so polite.
>
> But he never means anything serious till he talks about justice and right.
>
> When he stands like an ox in the furrow with his sullen set eyes on your own,
>
> And grumbles, 'This isn't fair dealing,' my son, leave the Saxon alone.

G.K. Chesterton's long poem *The Ballad of the White Horse*, published in 1911, was prophetic. In his 'Prefatory Note', he declared that King Alfred 'fought for the Christian civilization against the heathen nihilism', and that he gave the Romans and the Celts as well as the Saxons a part in Alfred's victory, for 'I fancy that in fact Alfred's Wessex was of very mixed bloods'. The poem tells the story of King Alfred's struggle for English freedom against the invading Danes:

A sea-folk blinder than the sea
Broke all about his land,
But Alfred up against them bare
And gripped the ground, and grasped the air,
Staggered, and strove to stand.

Anglo-Saxonism was used to underpin the development of English democracy, and Nordicism, by emphasising the Scandinavian rather than the Germanic roots of the English, helped to justify the increasing suspicion of the expanding German Empire.

6. Patriotic Anglo-Saxonism: Defending English Freedom

In the twentieth century England fought Germany in the two World Wars, and in the latter especially England's independence was at stake. Despite these wars, there was no disguising the German origins of the English people, but, because of them, there was perhaps an emphasis on the defence of English freedom.

1066 and All That (1930) took a typically English light-hearted view of English history. Its authors, **Walter Carruthers Sellar** and **Robert Julian Yeatman**, had served as subalterns in the First World War, and when the War ended they went up to Oriel College, Oxford, to study history. The authors state, 'In the year 1066 occurred the other memorable date in English History, viz. *William the Conqueror, Ten Sixty-six*'. Of course, 'The first date in English History is 55 B.C., in which year Julius Caesar (the *memorable* Roman Emperor) landed'. Chapter 2 is entitled *Britain Conquered Again,* and describes how 'The brutal Saxon invaders drove the Britons westward into Wales and compelled them to become Welsh'. Chapter 4 is also entitled *Britain Conquered Again,* and explains that 'The Danish Conquest was, however, undoubtedly a *Good Thing,* because although it made the Danes top nation for a time it was the cause of Alfred the Cake (and in any case they were beaten utterly *in the end* by Nelson)'. The authors imply that the English are determined never to be conquered again.

The film *The Adventures of Robin Hood* provided a Technicolor version of Anglo-Norman history for the generation of the Second World War. Starring Errol Flynn, Olivia de Havilland, Basil Rathbone, and Claude Rains, it was made by Warner Brothers in Hollywood in 1938, on the eve of the War. Written by Norman Reilly Raine and Seton L. Miller, it purports to be 'Based Upon Ancient Robin Hood Legends', but seems to owe a lot to Scott's *Ivanhoe.* It is set in an England divided between Normans, supporters of the usurping Prince John, and the downtrodden Saxons, loyal to King Richard the Lionheart. Robin Hood (Errol Flynn) rallies the Saxons in support of a 'free England', and Lady Marian (Olivia de Havilland) calls upon Norman and Saxon to live together in harmony.

The excavations at **Sutton Hoo** in 1938-39, again on the eve of the Second World War, provided concrete evidence of Anglo-Saxon art and culture, most expressively in the helmet with its face-like mask, perhaps the most vivid image from Anglo-Saxon times. The discovery of this treasure was the Anglo-Saxon equivalent of Schliemann's finds at Mycenae and Carter's in the Valley of the Kings. Displayed in the British Museum, the treasure, especially the continually reproduced image of the helmet, continues to resonate.

In the second half of the twentiety century the serious student of Anglo-Saxon history had a superb introduction in **Dorothy Whitelock**'s *The Beginnings of English Society* (1952), a volume of *The Pelican History of England*. Whitelock was educated at Leeds Girls' High School and Newnham College, Cambridge, where she read English. She went on to do research at Cambridge and at the University of Uppsala in Sweden. She returned to teach at Oxford and then to become Professor of Anglo-Saxon at Cambridge. The Second World War left no apparent trace on Whitelock's passionate interest in the Anglo-Saxon life for its own sake. Her declared intention was not 'to give an account of Anglo-Saxon political history, but to assemble ... what can be learnt about the ways of life of the English between their settlement in Britain in the middle of the fifth century and their conquest by the Normans'. She concluded that 'Quite apart, however, from any question of what they [the Anglo-Saxons] handed on to us, ...[they] are worthy of respect and study for their own sake'.

Having cut their teeth on Whitelock's work, students (and I was one of them) could then go on to try to chew over and to digest the solid bulk of F. M. **Stenton**'s *Anglo-Saxon England*, part of *The Oxford History of England*, first published during the war in 1943. There they would find the detailed political history that Whitelock had omitted. Stenton summed up his work thus:

> In political history the central interest ... is the evolution of an effective monarchy, covering all England, ... The volume ends with the death of William the Conqueror, who in twenty years had transformed this immemorial German kingship ....

He insisted that 'the men whose settlements formed the original English kingdoms all belonged to a single group of closely related German nations'. His judgement on the Norman Conquest was that 'to the ordinary Englishman ... the Conquest must have seemed an unqualified disaster', and he lamented that the Normans 'had produced little in art or learning, and nothing in literature that could be set beside the work of Englishmen. But politically they were the masters of their world'.

A few years later, in the middle of the Swinging Sixties, H. R. **Ellis Davidson** produced a scholarly celebration of Teutonic heathenism, *Gods and Myths of Northern Europe* (1964). Hilda Roderick Ellis Davidson came from the same mould as Dorothy Whitelock. She was educated at Park High School for Girls, Birkenhead, and Newnham College, Cambridge, where she studied English and archaeology. She gained a Ph. D. in 1940 with a study of Scandinavian heathenism. She taught English at the Royal Holloway College and then at Birkbeck College.

Davidson boldly declared that

> We have largely neglected however the mythology of our own forbears, the Anglo-Saxons and Vikings who settled in the British Isles and worshipped their gods there before Christianity came. I believe this to have been to our considerable loss ...

She then went on to list the virtues of these ancestors: courage, vigour, enthusiasm, loyalty, appreciation of fair dealings, respect for women, individualism, self-discipline, and the ability to 'accept adversity cheerfully without whining or self-pity'. One recognises the authentic tone of a grammar school education.

The most obvious Anglo-Saxonist product of the Second World War, was Churchill's *History of the English-Speaking Peoples* (1956-58). **Sir Winston Leonard Spencer Churchill** (1874-1965) was the son of an English aristocrat and his American wife. He served as a soldier and a journalist in the last British African colonial wars, entered parliament, and became a minister during the First World War, and then prime minister during the Second World War. He wrote accounts of his experiences in Africa, a life of his ancestor, the Duke of Marlborough, and histories of both World Wars. Churchill knew better than anyone that it was not England but America that had won the Two World Wars, or, as Sellar and Yeatman put it, 'America was thus clearly top nation'. The son of an American mother, Churchill believed that 'Language, law, and the processes by which we have come into being, already afforded a unique foundation for drawing together and portraying a concerted task,' and he looked forward to 'ultimate union'. For Churchill, Anglo-Saxon England was 'a kingdom, acknowledged by all who spoke the King's English', and 'on the whole the English doctrine was that a free man might choose his lord, following him in war, working for him in peace, and in return the lord must protect him against encroaching neighbours and back him in the courts of law'. These were the germs of democratic England and by extension not only the British Commonwealth but also the United States of America.

Perhaps the most popular English historian writing in the twentieth century was **Arthur Bryant** (1899- 1985). In the First World War he served as a pilot in the Royal Flying Corps. Bryant was a man of increasingly right-wing views. In 1939 he was one of a group of Englishmen who travelled to Germany to celebrate Hitler's fiftieth birthday, and after the outbreak of the Second World War he urged making peace with Germany and denounced Churchill as a warmonger. During the War, he produced a series of books about the Revolutionary and Napoleonic Wars. After the War he embarked on a series of books about the history of England. Bryant's Anglo-Saxons were 'great seamen, fighters and colonists', and 'they were great farmers'. 'Their form of government, though aristocratic, was far simpler and freer than that of Rome', for 'Though ready to enslave others, the English were great lovers of their own freedom'. This free government formed the basis of modern democracy, a direct line running 'From the Saxon Witenagemot to the twentieth century parliament, from the village hustings and manor court to the trade union lodge and parish council'. These Anglo-Saxons were not only free, but also 'green':

> "His coat", runs the old song, "is of Saxon green", and it is of a green-clad folk in a green land that we must think of them, swinging their axes and driving their ploughs through mysterious forest and dark earth to make the land we love.

This love of the green English land by those who still lived in the countryside and those who lived in the towns and cities, but usually sought to escape back to the countryside, was to be a strong element in the new, alternative Anglo-Saxonism that emerged in the later twentieth century.

The prophet of this popular Anglo-Saxonist revival was Tolkien. **J.R.R. Tolkien** (1892-1973) spent his working-life as a university lecturer, specialising in medieval English literature, though he had a love of all sorts of languages, both real and imagined. As Professor of Anglo-Saxon at Oxford, he made a major contribution to Anglo-Saxon studies with his *Beowulf: the Monsters and the Critics* (1936), arguing that *Beowulf* was a complete poem, not just a collection of fragments. Like many men of his generation, he had served in the First World War, and lived through the Second, in which his son also served. Indeed he was working on his masterpiece, *The Lord of the Rings* (1954-5) during the second war. Tolkien was not writing a *roman à clef*, in which there was a one-to-one correspondence between elements of his fictional world and the real world, and he rejected an allegorical interpretation of the work. Nevertheless, it is possible to see the Hobbits as the English and the Shire as England, menaced by hostile forces from beyond its borders. The Hobbits, however, with their quiet domestic virtues are, perhaps, the modern English. The Anglo-Saxons are to be found in Tolkien's Rohirrim with their heroic lifestyle and their alliterative verse:

Out of doubt, out of dark to the day's rising
I came singing in the sun, sword unsheathing.
To hope's end I rode and to heart's breaking:
Now for wrath, now for ruin and a red nightfall!

Tolkien blamed Hitler 'for ruining, perverting, misapplying, and making for ever accursed, that noble northern spirit, a supreme contribution to Europe, which I have ever loved, and tried to present in its true light'. At the beginning of the new millennium, Peter Jackson's epic film trilogy of *The Lord of the Rings* increased the interest in a book voted the best of the twentieth century.

If the twentieth century was the age of Modernism, in which English literature was represented in prose by Joyce and in poetry by Eliot, then Tolkien represents Counter-Modernism. If Joyce and Eliot were part of the avant-garde, then Tolkien was firmly within the derriere-garde. As he worked on *The Lord of the Rings,* while the fate of England and of Europe lay in the balance, English history had come full circle in reality and in fiction; it ended, as it had begun, in epic.

7. Post-modern Anglo-Saxonism: Re-Creating Anglo-Saxony

At the beginning of a new century and a new millennium, postmodernism has deeply affected cultural Anglo-Saxonism. Postmodernism declares that the modern age, the triumph of the rationalist Enlightenment is over, that a new, post-modern age has begun, Meanwhile a New Age, in the sense that rationalism has been abandoned, has been announced. As a result, a new, alternative Anglo-Saxonism has sprung up, attempting to re-create in the present the values of the mythical Anglo-Saxon past.

The academic discipline of Anglo-Saxonism, the study of Old English and of Anglo-Saxon society, explicitly conscious of its postmodern situation, remains productive but embattled. Scholars in the field continue to produce an increasing volume of work, including the monumental *Dictionary of Old English, The Sources of Anglo-Saxon Literary Culture,* and *Fontes Anglo-Saxonici* [The Sources of Anglo-Saxon] and a stream of books and learned articles, but like most academics they write for each other. The requirement, however, that English Literature undergraduates should study Old English has been abandoned, and Anglo-Saxon studies find themselves struggling for a place in a competitive academic market. Perhaps because of this, Anglo-Saxonists are acutely aware of the history of their discipline.

History as an academic discipline, perhaps because evidence is central to its methodology, remains largely immune to postmodernism in particular and to grand theory in general. The study of Anglo-Saxon history, however, must be threatened by the lack of undergraduate training in Old English and of the disappearance of Latin from secondary schools, together with the Hitlerisation of history in schools. Moreover, there seem as yet to be no successors to the works of Stenton and Whitelock as classics in the field, but a strong contender is **P. H. Sawyer**'s *From Roman Britain to Norman*

England, though Sawyer's bibliography acknowledges the continued role of Stenton and Whitelock. First published in 1978, and issued in a second edition in 1998, Professor Sawyer's book has been reprinted as recently as 2002. With its up-to-date bibliography, it is a successful attempt 'to interpret early English history in the light of recent research', and it looks set to become the new standard textbook. Professor Sawyer's evidential approach is demonstrated by his decision to start with the seventh century, when the earliest Anglo-Saxon written sources were produced and to work backwards and then forwards from there. Nevertheless, his work betrays the influence of postmodernism in so far as rather than seeking to construct a continuous narrative it concentrates on assessing the evidence. On doubtful or controversial issues, such as how and why the English language replaced the British, he is careful to consider all sides of the question. This approach is reinforced by a lengthy 'Postcript to the Second Edition', in which he revises his account in the light of further evidence, research, and publications. The serious student who wants a clear assessment of the latest research need look no further.

If television, because of the amount of film available from the twentieth century, is pushing the Hitlerisation of history, it also alerts viewers to earlier periods, and often ties in a television series with a book. **Michael Wood** has done much to popularise the history of earlier periods, including that of the Anglo-Saxons, and his *In Search of England* includes an essay on 'The Norman Yoke'. 'For the English', he writes, 'it has been the Norman Conquest which has been one of the greatest sources of myth', and he describes its manifestations in comic-strips, films, and Stenton's 'great book ... [which] was our bible in the sixth form'. He recounts his schoolboy encounter with Field Marshal Montgomery, an embodiment of the Normans, and outlines the development of the myth of the Norman Yoke. Finally, he puts into the mouth of an archaeologist a rhapsody for lost Anglo-Saxon England: "beautiful, archaic and idiosyncratic ... I don't think we ever forgot"'.

Richard Rudgley's *Barbarians: Secrets of the Dark Ages* is the book of the TV series. He accepts that 'Germanic roots are entangled in the fabric of English culture'. In particular, he points to the triumph of the English language, 'a major cultural transformation', which 'would have needed significant numbers of immigrants'. Rudgley's Anglo-Saxons are 'immigrants' rather than invaders, and he maintains that 'the migrants integrated fairly peacefully with the natives'. He also describes the archaeological evidence, which shows Germano-Scandinavian material culture replacing Romano-Celtic, and concludes that 'the indigenous people, preferred Anglian dress, fashions and designs'. Writing after a decade of wars of ethnic cleansing in Europe, Rudgley views the change from Roman Britain to Germanic England not so much as an invasion but more a change of fashion.

Francis Pryor, President of the Council for British Archaeology, expounds this revisionist view in his *Britain A. D.*, another book based on a TV series. He argues that the archaeology and the history of the period are 'irreconcilable', because the written sources are mainly 'polemic'. Accordingly most archaeologists no longer believe in 'large scale Anglo-Saxon mass migrations'. The change from post-Roman Britain to Anglo-Saxon England is 'caused by people changing their minds, rather than their places of residence', in other words more by "acculturation", than migration', 'It's not a question of invasion and takeover, but of attitude to life'. He sees the Anglo-Saxons as 'symbols to do with national identity' which 'have outlived their usefulness as symbols of that sort'. As a result, 'If we are looking for English origins, we should forget the "Anglo-Saxons" and turn instead to the resident population ... that diverse group of people – the British'.

A more traditional view of the Anglo-Saxon invasion is conveyed by **Terry Deary**'s *The Smashing Saxons,* part of the *Horrible Histories* published by Scholastic Children's Books. According to Deary, the Saxons 'invaded Britain ... They drove the Brits [sic] west into Wales and Cornwall. Then the Vikings ... tried to push the Saxons out. ... But in 1066 the Normans came across and took control. The Normans became the rulers and the Saxons became the peasants'.

In fiction the myth of the Norman Yoke is just as strong as ever. **Julian Rathbone**'s *The Last English King* is a historical novel about the rise and fall of Harold Godwinsson. It is a popular book; first published in 1997, it went into paperback in 1998, and was reprinted nine times in 1998, six times in 1999, and again 2000, and 2001. For Rathbone's characters, the Norman Conquest is "'a whole country ... betrayed to bondage and slavery for a thousand years'", and the Normans are "'A bunch of psychopaths ... the rulers of the English ... for ever' ... 'For a thousand years anyway'".

Perhaps the work of **Dr Brian Bates** best exemplifies postmodern Anglo-Saxonism with its alternative, New Age approach. A professor at the University of Brighton and past Chairman of Psychology at the University of Sussex, he teaches a course in Shamanic Consciousness. One can hear the sound of Hume and Gibbon turning in their graves. His novel *The Way of Wyrd* (1983) is about an Anglo-Saxon shaman, a tribal sorcerer who journeys into the unconscious. In *The Wisdom of the Wyrd* he offers 'a way of wisdom which once was ours a thousand years ago', believing that 'we need to rediscover the wisdom of our "native" heritage ...'. He seeks to return to 'the largely forgotten civilisation of the forest peoples of Europe, the Anglo-Saxon and Celtic tribal cultures ... and their ways of deep understanding which I have called the wisdom of the Wyrd'. By Wyrd, an Anglo-Saxon word, from which is derived the modern word 'weird', he means destiny, power, magic, prophetic knowledge, the unexplainable, the sacred, the grounding of existence, the life force, and he offers a set of techniques, culled from Anglo-Saxon lore, to access it. **Brian Rosebury**, in his *Tolkien: A Cultural Phenomenon*, examines the forms of the cultural afterlife of *The Lord of the Rings*, including relabelling, in which one cultural product is associated with another, and assimilation, in which the distinctive features of one work are located within another. Professor Bates relabels and assimilates his Wyrd with Tolkien's work in *The Real Middle Earth: Magic and Mystery in the Dark Ages*. He points out that 'stretching from Old England to Scandinavia and across to western Europe, there arose ... a largely forgotten civilization ... And it is this culture ... on which he [Tolkien] based *The*

Lord of the Rings'. Bates believes that 'the realm of human imagination is once again considered as important as our rational mind. We need both. Middle-earth has returned'. He embarks on a detailed account of Anglo-Saxon culture, and concludes that 'when we read about the real Middle-earth, we feel reconnected with ourselves'.

Postmodern Anglo-Saxonism, as well as Tolkienism, constitutes a cultural phenomenon, as various groups look back to the Anglo-Saxons both for inspiration and for validation. A wide variety of Anglo-Saxonism can be found in the printed literature and in the wild undergrowth of the Internet, ranging from the enthusiastic and the scholarly to the strange and the dangerous. They include the splendid Regia Anglorum, a society that attempts to recreate English life at the turn of the first millennium.

The extreme Right uses Anglo-Saxonism to appeal to fears of immigration and European integration. A search of the Internet for Hereward the Wake revealed a brief biography, which declares that Hereward is 'a symbol of resistance against foreign oppression' from 'the growing mass coloured immigration' and 'the European superstate', which 'will soon mean the end of us as a people', and concludes 'Let us flock to the cause of the watchful British National Party while there is time!'.

In contrast **Father Andrew Phillips**, an English Orthodox Christian priest and the author of a study of Barnes, makes a gallant attempt to use Anglo-Saxonism to appeal for reconciliation and a return to Orthodox Christianity, to 'find again in our hearts and minds the spiritual heritage of our fathers, ... to go and heal the wound of the Norman Invasion that has never healed, ...'. Fr Phillips sees the Norman Conquest as a spiritual catastrophe almost on a par with the biblical Fall of Man, but sees in the traditions of the Anglo-Saxon Church the means to heal that wound.

Fr Phillips's is a voice crying in the wilderness, a still small voice compared to the roar of the Heathen revival. As G. K. Chesterton remarked, 'When a man ceases to believe in God, he does not believe in nothing. He believes in anything'. The decline of Christianity does not necessarily lead to an increase in atheism. It can and does lead to a revival of **Heathenism** or Odinism or Asatru or the Northern Tradition. Postmodernism with its denial of any objective truth makes this possible. There has been a semantic shift in the verb 'to perceive', which once meant 'to understand the truth', but now means 'to hold a subjective opinion'. Having decided that Christianity is not true, some people seem to decide that they are Heathens, because Heathenism is as good as any other religion and it suits them. As Pete Jennings puts it in *The Pagan Federation Northern Tradition Information Pack,* 'people who have become interested in Paganism generally have sought out a path that they feel is part of their native cultural identity'. There are also those like **Edred**, the author of *Introduction to the Germanic Tradition,* who maintain that 'One is Germanic if one is of Germanic stock, and/or has grown up speaking a German language', and, hence, 'The Germanic tradition, for those who *are* Germanic, is not a choice ... but is a matter of *who* you really are'.

At the turn of second millennium, a thousand years after the Norman Conquest, we are in the midst of an Anglo-Saxon revival. It takes many forms, scholarly and popular, Christian and Heathen. Despite its occasional negative aspects, it remains a positive source for expressing the identity not only of the English in this island but also their children throughout the world.

Appendix
Democratic Procedure

Democratic procedure consists of a set of customary rules, which can be spelt out as standing orders.

- An elected *chairperson* enforces the rules, beginning with a prompt start.

- An elected *secretary* draws up and circulates the *agenda* and the *minutes* of the last meeting in advance of the meeting.

- The *agenda* is the list of the business of the meeting, i.e. things to be decided, usually in the form of *motions* (see below). The next to the last item is the time and place of the next meeting. The last item is *Any Other Business,* i.e. any business not on the agenda.

- The *minutes* are a record of decisions taken, i.e., motions carried or *resolutions* (see below), not of what is said.

- The *quorum* is the minimum number or proportion of members who need to be present, normally not less than one third.

- A *motion* is a proposal beginning with the word 'That', e.g. 'That this Anglo-Danish army fight to the last man'.

- A motion must be proposed by a *proposer* or *mover,* and must be *seconded* by another member.

- The chairperson then asks the proposer to speak in support of the motion.

- The seconder may speak next or later as he/she chooses.

- The chairperson then asks for an opponent of the motion to speak, and so on, until everyone has had a chance to speak. Although all may speak, all need not speak. Apart from the proposer who may speak again at the end of the debate, each member may speak ONLY ONCE on each motion. Members stand to speak, if they can.

- An *amendment* altering the terms of the motion may be proposed, seconded, and debated on as above. When all who wish to speak on the amendment have spoken, the chairperson puts the question to the vote by a show of hands. If there is a majority in favour, the amendment is carried. If the amendment is defeated the original motion stands.

- The chairperson then puts the amended or original motion to the vote by a show of hands. If carried by a majority, it becomes a *resolution*. If the voting is equal, the chairperson has a casting vote.

- Members may raise *points of order* if they think the rules of procedure are being broken, but the chairperson decides whether this is the case.

- The chairperson may order a member who is breaking the rules to leave. If he/she refuses to leave, the chairperson closes the meeting.

- A meeting may elect a *committee* to deal with details. Members of a committee remain seated to speak. Motions in committee do not require seconding, and members may speak more than once on each motion.

Bibliographical Notes

A useful bibliography of Anglo-Saxonism is available on the
World Wide Web in Simon Keynes, *Anglo-Saxon History: A
Select Bibliography*:
http://www.wmich.edu/medieval/rawl/keynes/biblios.htm .
For a concise history of the Anglo-Saxons, see John Blair, *The
Anglo-Saxon Age: A Very Short Introduction* (Oxford, 2000).
Michael Wood, *In Search of England: Journeys into the English
Past* (London, 2000) contains some stimulating essays on
Anglo-Saxonism. For detailed studies of the subject, see Carl.
T. Berkhout and Milton McC. Gatch (eds), *Anglo-Saxon
Scholarship: the first three centuries* (Boston, Mass, 1982), and
Allen J. Frantzen, *Desire for Origins: New Language, Old
English, and Teaching the Tradition* (London, 1990); see also
for comparison, Edward W. Said, *Orientalism* (Penguin edition,
London, 2003).

For historical, and literary, background, see the following:
Encyclopaedia Britannica (Standard Millennium Edition on
CD-ROM); *The Cambridge History of English and American
Literature* (18 vols, Cambridge, 1907-21) at
http://www.bartleby.com ; the various volumes of *The Oxford
History of England* and *The Pelican History of England*; John
Kenyon, *The History Men* (London, 1993); *The Dictionary of
National Biography* (21 vols, London, 1907-17); Da Engliscan
Gesipas [The English Companions] provide much information
at http://www.tha-engliscan-gesithas.org.uk ; Anglo-Saxon
Books, Frithgarth, Thetford Forest Park, Hockwold-cum-
Wilton, Norfolk, - http://www.asbooks.co.uk - publish a range
of relevant material.

For **Renaissance Anglo-Saxonism**, see Michael Wood, *In Search
of England: Journeys into the English Past* (London, 2000), and
Christopher Hill, *Puritanism and Revolution* (London, 1958);
for the Sarum use, the Anglo-Saxon liturgy, see Philip Baxter,
*Sarum Use: The development of a medieval code of liturgy and
customs* (Salisbury, 1994); Eamonn Duffy, *The Stripping of the
Altars: Traditional Religion in England c. 1400-c. 1580*
(London, 1992); Daniel Rock, *The Church of our Fathers* (3

vols, London, 1849-53); Daniel Rock, *The Church of our Fathers: A Selection* (Wigan, 1992); W. Maskell, *The Ancient Liturgy of the Church of England* (Oxford, 1882); Maskell, *Sarum Missal* (Cambridge, 1880); Maskell, *Monumenta Ritualia Ecclesiae Anglicanae* (3 vols, Oxford, 1882); Aidan Keller, *Old Rite Sarum Missal* (Austin, Texas, 2002); Percy Dearmer, *The Parson's Handbook* (12th edition, London, 1932); and http://www.smvph.org.uk/liturgy/history.php .

The classical Roman historians, together with Bede and *Beowulf,* are available in English translation as Penguin Classics: Caesar, *The Conquest of Gaul* (Harmondsworth, 1951); Tacitus, *On Britain and Germany* (Harmondsworth, 1948); Bede, *A History of the English Church and People* (Harmondsworth, 1955); *Beowulf* (Harmondsworth, 1957); for a wide range of relevant texts on-line, see http://www.sacred-texts.com/new/index.htm and http://sunsite.berkeley.edu/OMACL/ .

For **Enlightened Anglo-Saxonism**, the Enlightened historians are still in print: David Hume, *The History of England from the Invasion of Julius Caesar to the Revolution in 1688* (5 vols, Liberty Press edition, Indianapolis, 1983); Edward Gibbon, *The Decline and Fall of the Roman Empire* (6 vols, Everyman edition, London, 1994). For the philosophical background, see Norman Hampson, *The Enlightenment* (Harmondsworth, 1968).

For **Romantic Anglo-Saxonism**, Thomas Paine, *The Rights of Man* (Everyman edition, London, 1915), and Thomas Babington Macaulay, *The History of England from the Accession of James II* (3 vols, Everyman edition, London, 1906) can still be obtained cheaply second-hand; John Lingard, *The Antiquities of the Anglo-Saxon Church* (2 vols, Newcasle, 1806), Sharon Turner, *The History of the Anglo-Saxons from the Earliest Period to the Norman Conquest* (3 vols, London, 1828) and Francis Palgrave, *History of the Anglo-Saxons* (London, 1842) can be found in academic libraries, but Lingard's *History of England* (10 vols, London, 1830-50) in various editions can be obtained second-hand ; Sir Walter Scott, *Ivanhoe* (Wordsworth edition, Ware, 1995); E. J. Hobsbawm, *The Age of Revolution* (London, 1962) provides the best historical background.

For **Germanic Anglo-Saxonism**, there are clear explanations of the development of philology, in David Crystal, *Linguistics* (Harmondsworth, 1971); Anthony Burgess, *Language Made Plain* (London, 1975), re-printed as *A Mouthful of Air* (London, 1992); Burgess, 'Snow White and Rose Red' in *Urgent Copy* (Penguin edition, Harmondsworth, 1973). Thomas Carlyle, *Critical and Miscellaneous Essays* (6 vols, London, 1869) is to be found in academic libraries, but his *On Heroes, Hero-Worship and the Heroic in History* (London, 1895) is still to be found cheaply second-hand. John Mitchell Kemble's works are also to be found in academic libraries; they include *A Translation of the Anglo-Saxon Poem of Beowulf* (London, 1827); *Codex Diplomaticus Aevi Saxonici* (6 vols, London, 1839-48); *The Saxons in England: A History of the English Commonwealth till the Period of the Norman Conquest* (2 vols, London, 1849). Benjamin Thorpe's *Northern Mythology* has been re-printed by Wordsworth Editions (Ware, 2001).

For **Democratic Anglo-Saxonism**, see Andrew Phillips, *The Rebirth of England and English: The Vision of William Barnes* (Hockwold-cum-Wilton, 1996); Edward A. Freeman, *The History of the Norman Conquest of England* (6 vols, Oxford, 1867-79) in academic libraries; John Richard Green, *A Short History of the English People* (Everyman edition, 2 vols, London, 1915) available cheaply second-hand; Helen Dore (ed.) *The Earthly Paradise of William Morris* (no place, 1996) for the Preface to *The Volsung Saga*; Charles Kingsley, *Hereward the Wake* (Collins edition, London, 1954) is still in print. Some editions of Lewis Carroll's works, such as *Alice's Adventures in Wonderland and Through the Looking-Glass* (Pan edition, London, 1947), contain the original illustrations by John Tenniel. Kipling's *Puck of Pook's Hill* and his *Rewards and Fairies* can be obtained second-hand, but the former is available in a Penguin edition (London, 1994), and his verse is published as *The Works of Rudyard Kipling* (Ware, 1994) by Wordsworth. Chesterton's *The Ballad of the White Horse* is also available second-hand, can be found on the Internet, for example at www.gutenberg.org and is obtainable in new editions from the USA, such as the Ignatius Press edition, by way of amazon.com.

For **Patriotic Anglo-Saxonism**, see Walter Carruthers Sellar and Robert Julian Yeatman, *1066 and All That* (Penguin edition, Harmondsworth, 1960); for an account of Sutton Hoo, see Rugeley (see below); the standard Anglo-Saxon surveys are Dorothy Whitelock, *The Beginnings of English Society* (Harmondsworth, 1952), part of the *Pelican History of England*, F. M. Stenton, *Anglo-Saxon England* (London, 1947), part of the *Oxford History of England,* and H. R. Ellis Davidson, *Gods and Myths of Northern Europe* (Harmondsworth, 1964), another Pelican book; the popular histories include Winston S. Churchill, *A History of the English-Speaking Peoples* (Chartwell edition, 4 vols, London, 1956), Arthur Bryant, *The Story of England: Makers of the Realm* (London, 1953), re-printed as *The Medieval Foundation* (London, 1966); J. R. R. Tolkien, *The Lord of the Rings* (3 vols, London, 1954-55) has been re-printed in various editions; studies of Tolkien include Humphrey Carpenter, *J. R. R. Tolkien* (London, 1977), and Brian Rosebury, *Tolkien: A Cultural Phenomenon* (Basingstoke, 2003); the film trilogy of *The Lord of the Rings* is available on video and DVD, as is *The Adventures of Robin Hood.*

For **Postmodern Anglo-Saxonism**, Richard Appignanesi and Chris Garratt, *Postmodernism for Beginners* (Cambridge, 1995) provides an introduction to the theory; for academic history, see P. H. Sawyer, *From Roman Britain to Norman England* (London, 2002); for popular postmodern history, see Richard Rudgley, *Barbarians: Secrets of the Dark Ages* (London, 2002); for an accessible revisionist analysis of the archaeological evidence, see Francis Pryor, *Britain A.D.: A Quest for Arthur, England and the Anglo-Saxons* (London, 2004); for popular history for children, see Terry Deary, *The Smashing Saxons* (London, 2000); for Regia Anglorum, see http://www.regia.org ; for a postmodern novel about the Anglo-Saxons see Julian Rathbone, *The Last English King* (London, 1997); for alternative postmodern Anglo-Saxonism, see Brian Bates, *The Wisdom of the Wyrd* (London, 1996), and Bates, *The Real Middle-Earth: Magic and Mystery in the Dark Ages* (London, 2002); for English Orthodox Christianity, see Father Andrew Phillips, *Orthodox Christianity and the Old English Church* (no place, 1996), and http://www.orthodoxengland.org.uk, http://www.orthodox.clar.net/ , and http://www.antiochan-orthodox.co.uk/ ; for modern Heathenism, see Pete Jennings, *The Pagan Federation Northern Tradition Information Pack* (London, 1996, obtainable from the Pagan Federation, BM Box 7097, London, WC1 3XX), Edred, *Introduction to the Germanic Tradition* (Smithville, Texas, 2001), Wulfstan, *Odinism in the Modern World* (London, 2001), Brian Branston, *The Lost Gods of England* (London, 1957), Kathleen Herbert, *Looking for the Lost Gods of England* (Pinner, 1994).

Some other titles from Anglo-Saxon Books

An Introduction to the Old English Language and its Literature
Stephen Pollington

The purpose of this general introduction to Old English is not to deal with the teaching of Old English but to dispel some misconceptions about the language and to give an outline of its structure and its literature. Some basic knowledge about the origins of the English language and its early literature is essential to an understanding of the early period of English history and the present form of the language. This revised and expanded edition provides a useful guide for those contemplating embarking on a linguistic journey.

£4.95   A5   ISBN 1–898281–06–8   64 pages

First Steps in Old English
An easy to follow language course for the beginner
Stephen Pollington

A complete and easy to use Old English language course that contains all the exercises and texts needed to learn Old English. This course has been designed to be of help to a wide range of students, from those who are teaching themselves at home, to undergraduates who are learning Old English as part of their English degree course. The author is aware that some individuals have difficulty with grammar. To help overcome this and other difficulties, he has adopted a step-by-step approach that enables students of differing abilities to advance at their own pace. The course includes practice and translation exercises.

There is a glossary of the words used in the course, and 16 Old English texts, including the Battle of Brunanburh and Battle of Maldon.

£16-95   ISBN 1–898281–19–X   248 x 173mm / 10 x 6½ inches   256 pages

Ærgeweorc: Old English Verse and Prose read by Stephen Pollington

This audiotape cassette can be used in conjunction with *First Steps in Old English* or just listened to for the sheer pleasure of hearing Old English spoken well.
Tracks: 1. Deor. 2. Beowulf – The Funeral of Scyld Scefing. 3. Engla Tocyme (The Arrival of the English). 4. Ines Domas. Two Extracts from the Laws of King Ine. 5. Deniga Hergung (The Danes' Harrying) Anglo-Saxon Chronicle Entry AD997. 6. Durham 7. The Ordeal (Be ðon ðe ordales weddigaþ) 8. Wið Dweorh (Against a Dwarf) 9. Wið Wennum (Against Wens) 10. Wið Wæterælfadle (Against Waterelf Sickness) 11. The Nine Herbs Charm 12. Læcedomas (Leechdoms) 13. Beowulf's Greeting 14. The Battle of Brunanburh 15. Blacmon – by Adrian Pilgrim.

£7.50   ISBN 1–898281–20–3   C40 audiotape   Old English transcript supplied with tape.

Wordcraft   Concise English/Old English Dictionary and Thesaurus
Stephen Pollington

Wordcraft provides Old English equivalents to the commoner modern words in both dictionary and thesaurus formats. The Thesaurus presents vocabulary relevant to a wide range of individual topics in alphabetical lists, thus making it easily accessible to those with specific areas of interest. Each thematic listing is encoded for cross-reference from the Dictionary.

The two sections will be of invaluable assistance to students of the language, as well as those with either a general or a specific interest in the Anglo-Saxon period.

£9.95   ISBN 1–898281–02–5   A5   256 pages

The Rebirth of England and English: The Vision of William Barnes
Fr. Andrew Phillips

English history is patterned with spirits so bright that they broke through convention and saw another England. Such was the case of the Dorset poet, William Barnes (1801–86), priest, poet, teacher, self-taught polymath, linguist extraordinary and that rare thing – a man of vision. In this work the author looks at that vision, a vision at once of Religion, Nature, Art, Marriage, Society, Economics, Politics and Language. He writes: 'In search of authentic English roots and values, our post-industrial society may well have much to learn from Barnes'.

For the first time Saxon-English words created and used by Barnes have been gathered together and listed next to their foreign equivalents.

£4.95   ISBN 1–898281–17–3   A5   160 pages

English Heroic Legends
Kathleen Herbert

The author has taken the skeletons of ancient Germanic legends about great kings, queens and heroes, and put flesh on them. Kathleen Herbert's encyclopaedic knowledge of the period is reflected in the wealth of detail she brings to these tales of adventure, passion, bloodshed and magic.

   The book is in two parts. First are the stories that originate deep in the past, yet because they have not been hackneyed, they are still strange and enchanting. After that there is a selection of the source material, with information about where it can be found and some discussion about how it can be used. The purpose of the work is to bring pleasure to those studying Old English literature and, more importantly, to bring to the attention of a wider public the wealth of material that has yet to be tapped by modern writers, composers and artists.

Kathleen Herbert is the author of a trilogy, set in sixth century Britain, which includes a winner of the Georgette Heyer prize for an outstanding historical novel.

This title was previously published as *Spellcraft: Old English Heroic Legends*.

£9.95   ISBN 1-898281-25-4   A5   292 pages

The Anglo-Saxon Monastic Sign Language
Monasteriales Indicia
Edited with notes and translation by Debby Banham

The *Monasteriales Indicia* is one of very few texts which let us see how life was really lived in monasteries in the early Middle Ages. Written in Old English and preserved in a manuscript of the mid-eleventh century, it consists of 127 signs used by Anglo-Saxon monks during the times when the Benedictine Rule forbade them to speak. These indicate the foods the monks ate, the clothes they wore, and the books they used in church and chapter, as well as the tools they used in their daily life, and persons they might meet both in the monastery and outside. The text is printed here with a parallel translation. The introduction gives a summary of the background, both historical and textual, as well as a brief look at the later evidence for monastic sign language in England. Extensive notes provide the reader with details of textual relationships, explore problems of interpretation, and set out the historical implications of the text.

£4.95   ISBN 0–9516209-4–0   A5   96 pages

Latest Titles

Anglo-Saxon Attitudes – A short introduction to Anglo-Saxonism
J.A. Hilton

This is not a book about the Anglo-Saxons, but a book about books about Anglo-Saxons. It describes the academic discipline of Anglo-Saxonism; the methods of study used; the underlying assumptions; and the uses to which it has been put.

Methods and motives have changed over time but right from the start there have been constant themes: English patriotism and English freedom.

£6.95   A5   ISBN 1–898281–39-4   Hardback   64 pages

The Origins of the Anglo-Saxons
Donald Henson

This book has come about through a growing frustration with scholarly analysis and debate about the beginnings of Anglo-Saxon England. Much of what has been written is excellent, yet unsatisfactory. One reason for this is that scholars often have only a vague acquaintance with fields outside their own specialism. The result is a partial examination of the evidence and an incomplete understanding or explanation of the period.

The growth and increasing dominance of archaeological evidence for the period has been accompanied by an unhealthy enthusiasm for models of social change imported from prehistory. Put simply, many archaeologists have developed a complete unwillingness to consider movements of population as a factor in social, economic or political change. All change becomes a result of indigenous development, and all historically recorded migrations become merely the movement of a few hundred aristocrats or soldiers. The author does not find this credible.

£19.95   ISBN 1–898281–40-2   9 ¾ x 6 ¾ inches   245 x 170mm   Hardback   304 pages

A Departed Music – Readings in Old English Poetry
Walter Nash

The *readings* of this book take the form of passages of translation from some Old English poems. The author paraphrases their content and discuses their place and significance in the history of poetic art in Old English society and culture.

The authors knowledge, enthusiasm and love of his subject help make this an excellent introduction to the subject for students and the general reader.

£16.95   ISBN 1–898281–37-8   9 ¾ x 6 ¾ inches   245 x 170mm   Hardback   240 pages

Rudiments of Runelore
Stephen Pollington

The purpose of this book is to provide both a comprehensive introduction for those coming to the subject for the first time, and a handy and inexpensive reference work for those with some knowledge of the subject. The *Abecedarium Nordmannicum* and the English, Norwegian and Icelandic rune poems are included as are two rune riddles, extracts from the Cynewulf poems and new work on the three Brandon runic inscriptions and the Norfolk 'Tiw' runes.

Headings include: The Origin of the Runes; Runes among the Germans; The Germanic Rune Row and the Common Germanic Language; The English Runic Tradition; The Scandinavian Runic Tradition; Runes and Pseudo-runes; The Use of Runes; Bind Runes and Runic Cryptography.

£4.95 ISBN 1–898281–16–5 A5 Illustrations 96 pages

Rune Cards
Brian Partridge & Tony Linsell

"This boxed set of 30 cards contains some of the most beautiful and descriptive black and white line drawings that I have ever seen on this subject."

Pagan News

30 pen and ink drawings by Brian Partridge
80 page booklet by Tony Linsell gives information about the origin of runes, their meaning, and how to read them.

£9.95 ISBN 1-898281-34-3 30 cards & 80 page booklet – boxed

English Sea Power 871-1100AD
John Pullen-Appleby

This work examines the largely untold story of English sea power prior to the Norman Conquest. The author illuminates the much-neglected period 871 to 1100, an age when English rulers deployed naval resources, first against Norse Invaders, and later as an instrument of state in relations with neighbouring countries.

The author has gathered together information about the crewing, appearance and use of fighting ships during the period.

£14.95 ISBN 1-898281-31-9 9 ¾ x 6 ¾ inches 245 x 170mm 128 pages

Ordering

Payment may be made by Visa, or Mastercard. Telephone orders accepted.
See website for postal address
UK deliveries add 10% up to a maximum of £2-50
Europe – including **Republic of Ireland** - add 10% plus £1 – all orders sent airmail
North America add 10% surface delivery, 30% airmail
Elsewhere add 10% surface delivery, 40% airmail
Overseas surface delivery 5–8 weeks; airmail 5–10 days
For details of other titles and our North American distributor see our website or contact us at:

Anglo-Saxon Books

web site: www.asbooks.co.uk   e-mail: enq@asbooks.co.uk
Tel: 0845 430 4200   Fax: 0845 430 4201

Organisations

Þa Engliscan Gesiðas

Þa Engliscan Gesiðas (The English Companions) is a historical and cultural society exclusively devoted to Anglo-Saxon history. Its aims are to bridge the gap between scholars and non-experts, and to bring together all those with an interest in the Anglo-Saxon period, its language, culture and traditions. The Fellowship publishes a journal, *Wiðowind*. For further details see www.tha-engliscan-gesithas.org.uk or write to: The Membership Secretary, Þa Engliscan Gesiðas, BM Box 4336, London, WC1N 3XX, England.

Regia Anglorum

Regia Anglorum was founded to accurately re-create the life of the British people as it was around the time of the Norman Conquest. Our work has a strong educational slant. We consider authenticity to be of prime importance. Approximately twenty-five per cent of our members, of over 500 people, are archaeologists or historians. The Society has a large working Living History Exhibit and a forty-foot wooden ship replica For further information see www.regia.org or contact: K. J. Siddorn, 9 Durleigh Close, Headley Park, Bristol BS13 7NQ, England, e-mail: kim_siddorn@compuserve.com

The Sutton Hoo Society

Our aims and objectives focus on promoting research and education relating to the Anglo-Saxon Royal cemetery at Sutton Hoo, Suffolk in the UK. The Society publishes a newsletter SAXON twice a year. For information about membership see website: www.suttonhoo.org

Wuffing Education

Wuffing Education provides those interested in the history, archaeology, literature and culture of the Anglo-Saxons with the chance to meet experts and fellow enthusiasts for a whole day of in-depth seminars and discussions. Day Schools at Tranmer House, Sutton Hoo, Suffolk. Wuffing Education, 4 Hilly Fields, Woodbridge, Suffolk IP12 4DX, England education@wuffings.co.uk   web www.wuffings.co.uk   Tel. 01394 383908 or 01728 688749

Places to visit

Bede's World at Jarrow

Bede's world tells the remarkable story of the life and times of the Venerable Bede. Bede's World, Church Bank, Jarrow, Tyne and Wear, NE32 3DY Tel. 0191 489 2106; Fax: 0191 428 2361; website: www.bedesworld.co.uk

Sutton Hoo near Woodbridge, Suffolk

Sutton Hoo is a group of low burial mounds. Excavations in 1939 brought to light the richest burial ever discovered in Britain. Some original objects as well as replicas of the treasure are on display. National Trust - 2 miles east of Woodbridge on B1083   Tel. 01394 389700

West Stow Anglo-Saxon Village

An early Anglo-Saxon Settlement reconstructed on the site where it was excavated consisting of timber and thatch hall, houses and workshop. There is also a museum containing objects found during the excavation of the site. For details see www.stedmunds.co.uk/west_stow.html or contact: The Visitor Centre, West Stow Country Park, Icklingham Road, West Stow, Bury St Edmunds, Suffolk IP28 6HG   Tel. 01284 728718